THE
Archive Photographs
SERIES

TAVISTOCK

Tavistock Golf Club, 1911. In the year in which he won the fifth of his six Open Championships, Harry Vardon played the Tavistock course. He was the foremost British professional of his day and was the man who popularised the overlapping grip. In this exhibition match he helped the club to celebrate its twenty-first birthday. The ball that was used is preserved in the clubhouse.

THE
Archive Photographs
SERIES

TAVISTOCK

Compiled by
Gerry Woodcock

CHALFORD

First published 1997
Copyright © Gerry Woodcock, 1997

The Chalford Publishing Company
St Mary's Mill, Chalford,
Stroud, Gloucestershire, GL6 8NX

ISBN 0 7524 0760 0

Typesetting and origination by
The Chalford Publishing Company
Printed in Great Britain by
Redwood Books, Trowbridge

A late afternoon in the summer of 1922. A photographer standing on Abbey Bridge catches the scene as a lone schoolboy makes his way home across a deserted street. At the north end of Bedford Square a parade engages the interest of a few bystanders. There is only one motor vehicle in view, partly hidden behind the newly-dedicated war memorial.

Contents

Acknowledgements

My first word of thanks is to fellow-members of the Tavistock Local History Society. Individual colleagues have given me advice and support and the society's photographic archive, housed in the town museum, has been put at my disposal. The bulk of the pictures that I have used from this source originated in two collections. One was the work of William Merrifield, a pioneer local photographer in the third quarter of the nineteenth century. The other was the Kingdon collection, assembled by Eric Kingdon, a well-remembered newspaper editor and local historian. I am also very grateful to John Bodman for permission to use material from his extensive collection of postcards. The willingness of individuals and organisations to lend me photographs has been much appreciated and I would like to record my thanks to: Len Bird, Dee Boyce, Aidan Clotworthy, Jack Clotworthy, Bill Foster, Lenore Hicks, Trevor Kerswill, Kingdon House Community Association, Pat Mildren, John Olver, Michael Parriss, Philip Perry, John Philpott, Kathy Pym, David Sullivan, Tavistock Association Football Club, Tavistock Branch British Red Cross Society, Tavistock Golf Club, Tavistock Scout Group, *Tavistock Times Gazette*, Bill Tucker, Florence Watkins, Whitchurch Women's Institute and Thelma Wood. I also gratefully acknowledge the assistance willingly given by: Clifford Alford, David Anthony, Arthur Ball, Tony Bates, Norna Beadle, Elizabeth Cole, Su Davis, Julia Felles, Robin Fenner, Marjorie Greening, Audrey Howell, Barbara Howland, Alex Mettler, Sheelagh Parsons, Don Robinson, Don Sleep and Tony Wates. I hope that all those who helped me will share my pleasure at the appearance of this collection. I have done my best to check the accuracy of names, places and dates. I take responsibility for any errors that may have survived this scrutiny. This book is dedicated to the memory of the people of Tavistock whose doings are recorded in its pages.

Introduction

Tavistock, the settlement on the River Tavy, began its recorded life a thousand years ago. It was under the shadow of the great Benedictine Abbey, founded in AD 974, that the town was established, where the Fishlake, tumbling down the Billingsbear valley from its Hurdwick source, neared its destination, the right bank of the Tavy. In the thirteenth century this small community established a market, gained borough status, and began to send MPs to parliament. It remained, however, totally dependant on the wealth of the abbey, on the benevolence of monks, and on the will of the abbot. The closing of the monasteries in 1539 brought about a change of ownership. The monastic lands and properties were given by the King to John Russell, the ancestor of a long line of Earls, later Dukes, of Bedford. The dynasty continued to control the fortunes of the town until the early years of the twentieth century. Then, on the eve of the First World War, the Eleventh Duke of Bedford sold the bulk of his Tavistock property. Shops, houses, inns, offices, farms and open spaces were redistributed among a wide range of new owners, many of whom were former tenants. The local council bought a number of buildings and amenities and these have remained in public ownership. During this century the town lost the patronage of the Russells. It did not lose the indelible marks of the Russell era. The Bedford fingerprint remains, not only on the physical features of the town, but on many aspects of its institutional life. The imprint of the more distant centuries, when the patrons were the abbots, is rather less obvious, but still real.

The chronicler John Prince referred to Tavistock in 1701 as 'that fruitful seed-plot of eminent and famous men'. It has certainly produced some illustrious sons, notably Francis Drake, but also the poet William Browne and the jurist John Maynard. Schooled here were John Glanville, Speaker of the House of Commons on the eve of the Civil War, and W.H. Smith, bookseller and Victorian cabinet minister. The town has been represented in parliament by the likes of John Pym in the seventeenth century and Michael Heseltine in the twentieth. Among the much-travelled whose weary bones found a final resting-place in Tavistock were St Rumon and Edward Eyre, their deaths separated by 1,300 years.

In 1860 a locally published *Handbook for Tavistock* appeared. It contained an introductory historical chapter which took the story up to the visitation of the plague in 1626 and then broke off abruptly with the words: 'Nothing requiring special notice occurred in the town after that date'. The writer was reflecting the view that a long period of order, stability and tranquillity had descended on the community. The Civil War apart, there is, perhaps, some basis for this judgment. The authority of the church on the one hand and the duke's office on the other, though not unchallenged, generally held sway. The occasional election of an MP or a portreeve passed off, usually without incident and often without contest. The population remained more or less static, in terms of both size and mobility. The economy of the town seemed to be endlessly chugging along on the backs of the three traditional industries of tin, wool and agriculture. The first of these had given Tavistock the status of a stannary town. The second had left a physical symbol of its wealth in the form of a substantial addition to the parish church. The third sustained a regular pattern of market and fair activity. On all fronts the keynote appeared to be continuity. However, the author of the 'Handbook' was going beyond historical interpretation and was offering thoughts and hopes about the present and the future. Here he overlooked the enormous changes that were, at the time when he wrote, already well under way.

In the nineteenth century the town grew rapidly, in response to the development of the local mining enterprises. The population rose from 3,420 in 1801 to 8,912 in 1861, although it fell back thereafter as the copper boom collapsed and depression set in. Attempts from the late-nineteenth century on to deal with this situation, whether by such negative strategies as the encouragement of emigration, or by positive policies of fostering tourism, had limited success. Meanwhile, in the last half of the nineteenth century and the first part of this century, other fundamental changes were taking place. Improvements in transport and communications led not only to economic changes but to many modifications of everyday life. New patterns in the provision of education, health care, and welfare, brought other significant social changes. Other signs of the growth and deepening of community life came with the rapid increase in the number of clubs and societies, catering for all kinds of interests. Some of these organisations made possible, for the first time, a role for women in the public life of the town. This was also the age in which sporting activity became structured, with clubs being established and competitions organised. These economic and social changes had their reflection in political developments. A new system of elected and accountable local government emerged. As the grip of the duke and his establishment loosened and as more people got the vote, politics became livelier. Elections and loyalties were no longer predictable, levels of partisanship were high, and traditional authorities were being questioned. This was also happening in the field of religion. Already by the middle of the nineteenth century Sunday attendances at the six nonconformist chapels combined were exceeding the number who worshipped in the parish church. There were, finally and most obviously, the changes that were taking place to the face of Tavistock. Three modifications to the street pattern in the town centre took place. Plymouth Road was constructed to link Bedford Square with Fitzford. The town hall and market area was redeveloped, producing both the new Duke Street, and Market Road on land reclaimed from the Tavy. Drake Road provided, from 1890, access to the new railway station.

It is our good fortune that the camera made its appearance in time to record so many of these developments. Photography is a tool that helps us to explain what we were and thereby helps us to understand what we are.

One
The Setting

A deserted Guildhall Square as it appeared in the early years of the twentieth century. The Seventh Duke of Bedford, atop his granite pedestal, guards the Guildhall, built to his orders in 1848 to replace an earlier, dilapidated building in Bedford Square. It was used, not only as a courthouse, but for a whole range of civic and public meetings and functions. The square was part of the area in the town centre redeveloped by the Duke. It housed the police station, as it has continued to do. It also provided a home for the fire engine.

William Merrifield, the local librarian, was a pioneer photographer. In 1860 he took this picture of the riverside site to the east of Bedford Square. The area has been cleared of its slum properties, but the redevelopment, in the form of the construction of the Town Hall and the Pannier Market, has yet to begin. The buildings on Dolvin Road, principally the National School, are seen across the river.

One result of the redevelopment of the 1860s was to claim land that had hitherto formed one of two channels that the Tavy had taken to either side of a mid-river island. This land provided useful riverside access to the newly-constructed market and so a road was built on it, called Market Road. It is shown here soon after its construction.

Guildhall Square, *c.* 1880. The Duke's statue faces the administrative offices of the Bedford Estate, where most of the major decisions affecting the town were taken, and beyond that the Bedford Hotel. The square was used then, as later, for parking.

Bedford Square in 1910. The square then, as now, was dominated by the Town Hall. Officially opened in February 1864, its façade, with its green Hurdwick stone, had been seen to good effect twelve months earlier, when the building had been illuminated as part of the festivities to mark the wedding of the Prince of Wales. To the right of the hall is Court Gate, one of four entrances to the precinct of Tavistock Abbey. It underwent major restoration in the nineteenth century.

Bedford Square in 1881. The range of buildings on the northern side of the square present an unfamiliar vista because there is, as yet, no Drake Road. Access to Barley Market Street was via an alley, the entrance to which was the covered passage visible under the *Gazette* building. This was Post Office Lane, the original home of the town's post office.

The foreground of this 1881 picture shows the foot of Whitchurch Road, the original route out to the south and referred to on Victorian maps as the Old Plymouth Road. On the left is the access road to the goods yard of the Great Western Railway station. Beyond is the recently-widened Abbey Bridge leading to Bedford Square.

In 1890 the London and South Western Railway Company opened its new line through Tavistock. The problem of providing suitable access to the new station was solved by constructing a new road out of Bedford Square. Drake Road was born. In this picture, taken in the year of the changes, a small group in the distance admire the new thoroughfare, while in the foreground a strangely assorted quartet stare rather uncertainly at the photographer.

Sacrificed at the birth of Drake Road were half of the Gazette office and whole of the adjacent property. Post Office Lane was also a casualty. Here, in 1910, the foot of the new road is flanked on the one side by Thomas Greenfield's reduced newspaper premises and on the other by Elizabeth Cole's restaurant. The immediate area remains, temporarily, a bank-free zone.

Tavistock derives its location and its name, from the river. Here, in 1900, is a largely unchanged scene of the Tavy between Abbey Bridge and the entrance to the Meadows. On the left is the wall marking the southern limit of the abbey precinct and the two-storey Still Tower, in which generations of monks distilled their potions. The river level suggest that there has been a period of dry weather.

The Tavy passes through the Meadows towards West Bridge. This stretch has always provided a popular walk. Here, in 1910, mothers or nannies give their charges an airing. The iron footbridge over the river had been erected in 1904 and carried a sewer. The Duke of Bedford had contributed £100 towards the £203 which was the total cost of the bridge.

From time to time, when heavy rain or melting snow on Dartmoor has overfed it, the Tavy swells. On this occasion, in August 1938, a crowd gathers near Abbey Bridge to watch the river's tantrums. This spot also marks the point at which, since 1805, water has been drawn off to supply the Tavistock Canal.

The old weir was destroyed in the flood of 1890. Here, in the same year, its replacement is under construction. The *Tavistock Gazette* called the new weir 'the lasting and conspicuous memorial to the great flood'. Abbey Bridge, in the background, was built in 1763 to carry the turnpike road to Plymouth. It was widened, and partially rebuilt, in 1860, to improve access to the G.W.R. station.

George Budge was a professional ironmaster who ran, in turn, foundries at Lumburn and at Tavistock. He was also an amateur, but very proficient, photographer. Among the images he has left are two photographs taken in about 1920. In all likelihood they feature members of his family, and the young lady who appears in both could well be Esther, his grand-daughter. The first one, which he called 'Looking North', is a view of the town and beyond with Fitzford church in the foreground, and is taken from Crease Lane.

The second picture of the pair, which Budge labelled 'Looking South', is taken from a field above the Old Exeter Road. In the foreground the LSWR line crosses the road. Behind, a panorama of the town centre features two well-loved landmarks, the tower of St Eustachius and the spire of the Congregational church. The latter was to be demolished in 1960.

A Merrifield photograph from 1862, showing the north side of Plymouth Road from Bedford Square to Russell Street. The Bedford Hotel casts its shadow across the road. On the corner of Russell Street stands the Grammar School which opened twenty-four years earlier. The churchyard presents a rather more wild appearance than a later age would consider appropriate.

A view of the western part of the town, seen from the church tower in the 1890s and covering Plymouth Road from the vicarage to Fitzford.

Looking east from the church tower in 1927. The centrepiece here is the area of Victorian redevelopment. The rectangular site is bounded to south and north by the river and by Duke Street, and comprises the Town Hall, the Pannier Market, Market Road and the Duke Street shops. The limit of the area is clearly indicated as the point where the broad, straight Duke Street becomes the narrow, curving Brook Street.

An aerial view taken from a point above the Town Hall in about 1950. Particularly featured is the sweep of West Street from the parish church to the foot of Spring Hill. The two Methodist churches, in Chapel Street and Russell Street, appear prominently, as does the Carlton cinema, erected in 1939.

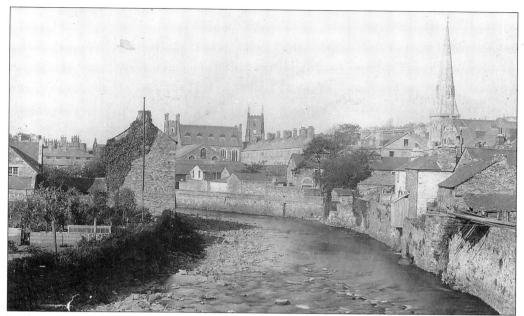

Looking west from Vigo Bridge in 1895. The bridge was built in 1773 to carry traffic to the turnpike road across Dartmoor to Moretonhampstead. The name derives from some nearby property, which in turn commemorated Drake's daring attack on that Spanish port. Three hundred yards downriver was Tavistock's original bridge, built in the 1260s and surviving until the 1760s.

The town as seen from Deerpark in 1911. The name 'Deerpark' records the use to which the abbots of Tavistock Abbey put this area. Edward Rundle, the Duke of Bedford's steward, had a house built here. Below him and on the corner of Dolvin Road and Whitchurch Road (in the picture's foreground) was the Bedford Yard, the focus of all the building and maintenance operations with which Rundle and his master were involved.

West Street in the early years of the twentieth century. In the foreground is the foot of Rocky Hill, previously known as Cake's Hill. The footway alongside, now called Glanville Avenue, was then the Tunnel (top two-thirds) and the Town Steps (lower part). A feature of the end-wall of the house at the bottom of the Town Steps is a stone figure, partly covered in the picture but since fully revealed. Representing 'Law', it began life by helping to decorate the Crystal Palace during the Great Exhibition of 1851.

Duke Street in 1920. On the left of the picture, occupying the upper storey behind the balcony, is the Conservative Club, opened in 1896. The Midland Bank had, in 1915, come to nestle under it. The bank was to be joined, over the next few years, by all its main competitors. On the other side of Mr Kitchens' emporium is the Newmarket Hotel, which closed in the 1970s. The photographer has caught a moment of waiting, but it is not clear what people are waiting for. Traffic does not appear to be an imminent threat.

Looking westward along Duke Street in 1907. On the left, behind the advertisements for tea and cocoa, is the grocery store founded by John Carter in 1881 (see p. 100).

The main west-east shopping artery begins at the top of West Street and ends at the bottom of Brook Street. Brook Street contained a large number of businesses when this picture was taken in 1912. On the right is the Tavistock Hotel, run by William Follard. The inn, which dates from 1894, had behind it a brewery that was to operate up to 1926. On the opposite side of the road is Margaret Bray's recent-opened confectionery shop.

Pym Street in 1890. This area contained some of the oldest properties in the town. The young lady is standing outside the Temperance Hotel, opened in 1838 and closed in 1928, before being transformed, in turn, into council offices and public house. Behind her is Bank Square, on the western side of which is the Exeter Inn, a hostelry at the time second in importance only to the Bedford Hotel. In 1946 it became the British Legion Club.

King Street, c. 1890. More interesting, perhaps, than the performing bear, or his trainer, or the attendant urchins, are two features of the street. Firstly on the right, Madge Lane begins its climb to Glanville Road by passing under part of No. 1, King Street. Secondly, the old Union Inn and two former taverns mark the site to be occupied, from 1918, by the new Union Inn.

Madge Lane, *c.* 1900. This narrow, steep hill derives its name from its position on the route westward out of the town towards the house of St Mary Magdalen, a leper hospital that occupied a site later to be known as Mount Ford. Near the foot of the lane, the building shown on the opposite page extends across it, leaving a low passage-way beneath. On the high ground to the left, the top of the new railway viaduct and the station bridge can be seen.

Market Street, 1917. The town's oldest street was, for centuries, the setting for its many market activities. It lay at the centre of the medieval settlement that grew up outside the gates of the abbey. Market Street remained the commercial heart of the town until the latter half of the nineteenth century, when, with the Duke's redevelopment, the centre of gravity began to shift towards Duke Street.

Plymouth Road, 1910. This long, wide boulevard linking Guildhall Square and Fitzford was one of the most impressive features of the 'new Tavistock' to emerge from the mid-nineteenth century changes. On the left, the stately presence of the Bedford Estate office, the Bedford Hotel, and the vicarage, finally gave way to the open spaces of the Meadows. On the right, after the church, there were two imposing schools and a range of dignified villas.

Dolvin Road, 1910. The name commemorates the Godolphin family, who owned land hereabouts. On the right, next to the Bedford Yard, is the long-time home of the Collacott family, who produced generations of craftsmen and pillars of the church. Beyond lies the Victorian graveyard, already full when this picture was taken and superseded by the new cemetery on Plymouth Road.

In the fifteenth century the Fitz family, a well-known Tavistock dynasty, built themselves a mansion to the west of the town, By 1869, when this picture was taken, nothing of it remained except the derelict gatehouse. In that year what was left of the gatehouse was demolished, to be rebuilt two years later on the original site. The remains of the mansion itself had been removed a few years earlier to make way for the workers' cottages provided by the duke and seen here behind the gatehouse to either side.

The Fitzford mansion was built, as its name implies, close to a ford. This was, in the sixteenth century, replaced by a bridge. West Bridge is seen here in about 1900. Alongside are the Westbridge cottages, built in the middle of the nineteenth century and complementing the range at Fitzford across the river. The bridge was demolished and rebuilt in 1940.

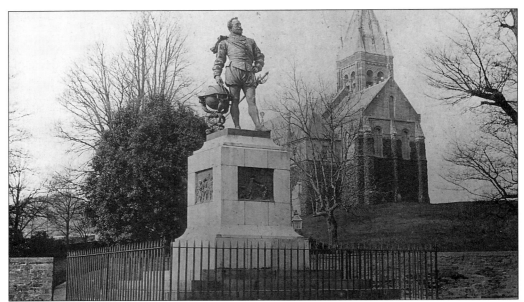

Sir Francis Drake is Tavistock's most famous son. He was born in 1542. The statue, the work of Joseph Boehm, was unveiled in September 1883, about twenty years before this photograph was taken. The hero stands ten feet tall, on a twelve feet high pedestal which contains three bas-reliefs depicting moments in his career. He is overlooked by Fitzford church, which pre-dates the statue by just sixteen years. There are no other buildings in sight.

Betsy Grimbal's Tower. One of the four entrances to the site of the medieval abbey, this tower changed little in appearance over a long period on either side of the 1894 date when it was photographed. Betsy Grimbal, alas, never existed. The building commemorates the Blessed Grimbald, a ninth century saint much revered by members of the Benedictine Order. The remains of the abbey are not extensive and this ruined building is one of the most potent reminders of an institution that flourished here from 981 to 1539.

Whitchurch, *c.* 1900. A large rural parish with a village centre, Whitchurch is shown here as separated from Tavistock by quite a lot of green countryside. Its church and school are on top of the hill. Yet its village character is soon to be threatened. Ribbon development along Whitchurch Road would be given impetus by the opening, in 1906, of the halt on the G.W.R. line and the spread of motor transport would give further momentum to this process of suburbanisation.

Walreddon Manor in 1922. The house, two miles due south of the town centre and in Whitchurch parish, was built in about 1550. It has two parallel wings. The western half was much modified in the eighteenth century. Among its illustrious occupants was Lady Mary Howard, who was born here in 1596 and who, on her death in 1671, left it to her cousin Sir William Courtenay. The Courtenays owned it thereafter until 1953. Edward Eyre, explorer and colonial adminstrator, lived here in retirement from 1874 until his death in 1901. He is buried in Whitchurch churchyard.

Kilworthy House, *c.* 1900. Kilworthy is the same age as Walreddon. For 200 years it descended through the Glanvilles, who had it built, and the Manatons, and was then, in 1771, bought by the Duke of Bedford. For a time in the nineteenth century it housed a school. The duke sold it in 1911 to Sir John Spear MP. In 1963 it became, once again, a school. The Glanville family also maintained a town house, in Pym Street.

Abbotsfield House in 1951. Abbotsfield was a much more recent addition to the ranks of Tavistock's stately homes than Walreddon or Kilworthy. It was built in 1853 for Thomas Morris, managing director of the Devon Great Consols Mining Company. After his death in 1885 it passed through a number of hands. During the Second World War it was used as military headquarters and was the setting in 1944 for a conference of British and American commanders, including Montgomery and Eisenhower. In 1951 it became a youth hostel and in 1984 a retirement home.

Two
Working

Photography, the preserve in the middle of the nineteenth century of talented amateurs like William Merrifield, had, by the end of the century, become a profession. Samuel Gimblett established himself in Market Street and Stanley Wadge in Brook Street. The most prolific of these early photographic businesses operated out of No. 1 West Street. Here Thomas Pearce had run a chemist's shop since the 1880s. With his two brothers, he developed the photographic side of the business. Here, in the family garden, on the eve of the First World War, are the three Pearce brothers, Sydney, Arthur and Thomas.

The Wharf in 1905. During the copper boom of the first half of the nineteenth century, this setting would have been one of noise and movement, with the waterside and the attendant warehouses reflecting all the bustle and activity of a small but thriving inland port. The four and a half mile canal, which had since 1817 linked Tavistock to the Tamar, was closed in 1873 and the wharf quickly became little more than a visible reminder of former glories.

The boom years of the mid-nineteenth century produced a range of industrial activities in support of the mining enterprises. This included, at one stage, three working iron foundries, at Parkwood, Mount Tavy and Lakeside. Thomas Nicholls, John Williams and Joseph Mathews ran the Bedford Iron Works in Lakeside from 1848 to 1866. The building retains essential features of its original function.

The decline of mining and manufacturing led to a switch in the local economy towards service industries. In 1899 two brothers, John and Edwin Spooner, built the Tavistock and District Laundry, off Parkwood Road. Long periods of ownership by William Gulley and by Lord Carnock brought it through to the 1970s, when it fell victim to the dual thrust of the domestic washing machine and the town centre launderette. It was photographed days before its demolition in 1989.

Merrivale Quarry, 1900. Quarrying is one local industry to have survived, although on a scale modest by nineteenth century standards. Merrivale granite has a national reputation. The quarry was opened in 1876. The stone was originally carted by road to the railway at Tavistock. In the early part of the twentieth century some 150 men were employed in the enterprise.

The Cattle Market in 1859. The market had for centuries been held on this riverside site, near Abbey Bridge and in the area to be known as Guildhall Square. Here is recorded the last occasion. In 1859 the market transferred to its site over the river, which offered more space and was conveniently near the recently-opened railway station.

The Cattle Market in 1920. At the new cattle market, off Whitchurch Road, Jan's Fair is being celebrated. Jan's (or St John's) Fair was the town's oldest fair, originating in a grant of 1116, and remained the only one until four others were established in the sixteenth century. It was held in August. The next one on the calendar was the Michaelmas Fair, the forerunner of Goose Fair, which was sometimes nicknamed 'St Joan's Fair', to distinguish it from St John's.

An annual event that draws crowds of spectators, as well as those professionally involved, is the pre-Christmas fatstock show. It was traditionally held in the Pannier Market. Here, in the early 1980s, is one of the last such occasions before the show's removal to more spacious accommodation.

Sidney Horrell was born at Buctor. He began showing Dartmoor ponies in 1920. His most lucrative exhibit was his pony stallion 'Peter Tavy II', winner of the championship at the Royal Show in 1965. The same pony, sharing the spotlight here with his owner, won prizes at the Devon County and Bath and West Shows, before being exported to Germany.

Plymouth Road in the 1880s. Labourers pause for the camera, with the Meadows in the background. The digging and winding gear suggests the laying of pipes, for either water or sewage. Responsibility for the town's sewers was transferred in 1876 from the Duke of Bedford to a Parish Sanitation Committee. The water supply was revolutionised by the opening of the Kilworthy Waterworks in 1865.

Plymouth Road in 1902. The scene is the construction of a new bridge taking the road over the canal. The builders did not have to consider the needs of any waterborne traffic, since the canal was by now defunct. The Fitzford cottages form the background.

Taylor Square, *c.* 1920. Looking northwards from the square towards Lakeside, the camera records some major road works. They may relate to the Fishlake, the stream taking this route that had, by this time, following some flood alerts, been consigned to an underground storm-pipe.

The Weir, 1961. A project which was carried out involved the provision of a concrete apron below the salmon ladder, which is to the left of the weir.

Samuel Gimblett took this picture in 1904. It shows the old gas works in the last year before its closure. The Tavistock Gas Company had been producing gas on this site, near the foot of Gas House Lane, later to be renamed Maudlin's Lane, since 1832. Absolem Francis surveys the scene. A director of the company since 1874, he has been, from 1891, secretary and manager of the enterprise.

Gimblett captures the staff of the old gas works in 1904. Absolem Francis is on the left. Production at the plant had increased steadily, reaching 18 million cubic feet in 1900. However, the premises were cramped, the equipment had become dated and electricity was emerging as a rival. New investment and a reconstruction of the company could not be undertaken without closing the works and finding a more flexible site.

The new gas works were sited in the Westbridge area, near the bottom of Pixon Lane and were opened in May 1906. This picture records the attendance at the opening ceremony. Standing centrally, hat in right hand and cigarette in left, is Henry Doble, chairman of the company. To his left are his fellow-directors: John Friend, John Buckley, Frank Pethybridge, Thomas Doidge, Arthur Bate, Stephen Nosworthy and, inevitably, Absolem Francis.

The gas works staff in 1953. Standing, left to right: Mike Parriss, Eric Sowton, Jack Eastlake, Robert Parriss, Bert Eva, Jack Westlake. Seated: Hilda Davey, Peggy Dunkley, Freda Short, Winnie Mudge, Sheila Ball. The company was nationalised in 1949. Gas production at the Tavistock plant ended in 1956. In 1959 the local council bought the works and converted them into an abbatoir.

Two postmen outside the post office, *c.* 1910. The original location of the town's post office was the narrow snicket known as Post Office Lane that connected Bedford Square and Barley Market Street. In 1859 it moved into the premises shown here, from where, in spite of recurrent proposals, it has not moved.

This general stores occupied a corner-site in Whitchurch at the junction of Horrabridge Road and Anderton Lane. In the early part of the century it was run by Maria Creber, grandmother of Norman Creber, the long-time head of the Duke Street business. Between the wars the proprietors were, successively, Mr S.J. Toye and Mrs E.V. Wilton. Mr Toye, who was also a builder, is seen here in about 1920, raising the roof of his new property. After the Second World War it became solely a private house and was known eventually as Pooh Corner.

Three
Playing

The Meadows, shown here in 1900, is a substantial area of open land between Plymouth Road and the river, stretching from the wharf to Fitzford. Since time immemorial townspeople have used it is as a place in which to stroll, play and meet. It was, however, private property, owned by the Duke of Bedford, who let it out as a hay meadow and for grazing. When in the 1860s the tenant tried to confine access to the banks of the river and the canal, local people felt it to be an attack on their customary rights. A campaign was launched to have the Meadows designated a public park.

Two ladies taking a rest in the Meadows, which then, in 1899, was still referred to by its old name 'Jessop's Hay'. In the previous year the Urban District Council had become the new tenant and had taken the first steps towards making the area a municipal park. The process was to take a further step in 1911 with its purchase by the council and its re-designation as a 'pleasure ground.'

The Meadows, c. 1950. Featured are some of the additions and improvements that came in the 1930s, particularly to mark George V's jubilee in 1935. They include the paddling pool and the bandstand, as well as trees, shrubs and seats.

Members of the Tavistock Cycling Club on the eve of the Second World War. The club had been founded in the 'golden age of cycling' in the last quarter of the nineteenth century, but had lapsed in 1914, when so many members went to the war. It was revived in 1934 under the name 'Tavy Wheelers'.

Before the First World War, the Cycling Club organised, on August Bank Holiday Monday each year, an athletics meeting, held at the sports field at the top of Green Lane. Here is the 1909 occasion, with the ladies' egg-and-spoon race getting under way, watched, it seems, by an almost exclusively male gallery.

This 1919 picture of the members of the Tavistock Sir Francis Drake Bowling Club was taken within five years of the formation of the club. Back row, left to right: J. Goss, S. Miles, H. Almond, W. Warren, S. Stapleton. Middle row: C. Pascoe, J. Pearce, W. Eddy, J. Whittome, T. Thraves, C. Warren, H. Thynne, S. Rayment, A. Callaway, W. Parsons, J. Williams. Front row: Mr Almond's son, J. Camozzi, T. Glanville, T. Ratcliffe, H. Priestly Shires, J. Snow, J. Heyden, H. Thynne, J. Minhinnick.

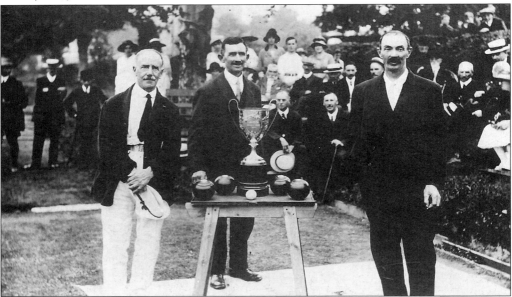

The Bowling Club's oldest trophy was first presented on this occasion in 1919. It was given in memory of Ernest Warran, who had been the club's chairman at the time of his death in 1918. He had also been clerk to the Urban District Council. Jonathan Snow, who succeeded him as chairman and who was headmaster of the Dolvin Road school, stands behind the cup. On the left is H. Priestly Shires, the first winner, who was also the club captain. On the right is T. Thraves, the runner-up.

A cool, damp April afternoon in 1926. The Bowling Club launches another season. The assembly of members and families is augmented by a few tennis players, who have drifted over to take part in the occasion. Sitting on the bank to the left of the flag-post are Jonathan Snow (chairman) and Joseph Heyden (a future chairman).

Mr Sperling's Harriers, 1911. In 1880 a subscription pack known as the Lamerton Harriers was formed, and in 1886 H.M. Sperling became its master. The pack continued to bear the master's name even after he had retired following an accident in the field in 1909. A favourite meeting point, as here, was outside the Bedford Hotel. In 1913 the pack was to be bought by Clarence Spooner and to become Mr Spooner's hounds.

20 June 1923. On this day in midsummer, very few seem to be on the streets of Tavistock as Turner's Tours scoop up about 150 townspeople intent on a day of sunshine and sand. The destination is Bigbury-on-Sea.

A Tavistock Cricket Club XI containing some pre-war heroes, 19 June 1937. Back row, from left to right: Bill Martin (scorer), Bill Rankin, Fred Barkell, Gordon Parry, Bill Colling, Len Avery, Glanville Davey (umpire). Middle row: Frank Millman, Eric Davey, Bill Fellowes, Doug May. Front Row: Frank Bond, Maurice Avery. The result was a victory over Holsworthy, made possible by an opening stand of 120 between Parry and Colling. Davey took 6 for 43 and Avery 4 for 57.

The Ring, on Whitchurch Down, has been the home of Tavistock Cricket Club since the club was founded in 1849. Here, in 1949, the team takes the field in a special centenary game. From left to right: D. Treloar, E. Stockbridge, M.C. Avery, D. Gordon, E. Davey, G.H. Parry (captain), J.D. Wedd, S.W. Colling, R. Forbes, W.M. Elderton. Hidden, or late taking the field, is F. Millman.

In more recent years major improvements have been carried out at the Ring, to both ground and pavilion. There has also been considerable success on the field. Here is the team that won the county cup in 1971, pictured before the final tie at Paignton. Back row, from left to right: Derek Pethick, Tony Clapp, Steve Callow, Hilton Jones, David Ewings, Phil Treseder, George Forbes (scorer). Front row: Geoff Husband, Maurice Craze, Doug Treloar, Tim Redman, Eric Jarman, Ray Tresedar (twelfth man).

The Tennis Club began its life at Whitchurch in 1921. Its premises at Anderton Lane offered only two grass courts, until 1956, when the first hard court was opened. Here, celebrating that event are: Harry Mudge, Jimmy Angell, Roy Curtis and Ken Watkins.

A second hard court followed in 1967. Mrs Mercy, the wife of the club's president, bank manager Ernest Mercy, performed the ceremony. Here she accepts flowers from Janet Watkins, whose father, club captain Ken, looks on. On the left is Mrs Doidge, the club secretary.

The courts at Anderton Lane were alongside the railway embankment. A picture from 1948 shows Joan Doidge playing as a train on the GWR line passes behind her. The club's move to the Meadows came in 1983.

The canal, closed to commercial traffic since 1873, has occasionally been used for pleasure boating. Here, in 1909, interest focuses on a playful echo of the national campaign then being waged to increase the size of the battleship fleet in competition with that of Germany. Tavistock's 'Dreadnought', armed to the teeth, prepares to sail off from the wharf.

The Tavistock Association Footbal Club was born in 1888. Its early years, in spite of not having a settled home, were very successful. In the late 1890s, for example, it put out strong teams including county players, and attracted large crowds to its Torland ground. On a stormy Easter Monday afternoon in 1898, this team defeated Surrey Wanderers 2-1, with Williams scoring both goals. Back row, left to right: Bickford, Lang, Northey. Middle row: Cole, Holman, Dockett. Front row: Merrifield, Williams, Kerswill, Sargeant, Knott.

When King George VI visited the town in December 1937, he presented a cup for competition at the Fatstock Show. Receiving it on behalf of the organisers is the show's president, Herbert Langsford. Langsford was co-owner of Pitts Cleave Quarry and a local councillor. He became chairman of the football club. In 1947 he bought land at Crowndale and presented it to the club. It has, since then, been the home of football in Tavistock and bears his name.

In September 1949 the Tavistock Hockey Club was launched and its Birchwood Terrace ground officially opened. Players and officials who gathered at the inauguration included, standing: Basil Margrett, Nick Stevens, Neil Solomon, Bill Bartholomew, Bernard White, George Golding, Bill Barnes, Jim Boddy, Bob Redman, Fred Tucker (umpire). Sitting: Hugh Treloar (trustee), Captain Garlick (president), Mrs Garlick, Captain Marrison (chairman), Stanley Willis (council chairman), Ted Maunder (trustee) with Master Maunder, 'Charles' Charleston, Olaf Nelson.

From the outset the club provided for both men and women members. Here, in 1949, Mrs Garlick, wife of the club's president, is surrounded by players. Standing: Ruth Bawden, Jill Spiller, Inez Martin, Rita George, June Bickford, Mary Peek, Miss Sanders, Pat Ford, Jane Marrison, Jacqui Davis, Roma Ford, Marion Hartley, Betty Hussey. Sitting: Jean Nosworthy, Mary Boddy, Pam Furse, Florence Doidge. Kneeling: Two junior Marrisons, sister and dog.

The Golf Club was founded in 1890, when the Duke of Bedford gave permission for a course to be laid out on Whitchurch Down. From the earliest days women were welcomed as members. In 1903 a Mr Still of Walreddon gave a cup to be competed for county-wide. Tavistock were the first winners. Mrs Still sits behind her husband's trophy. The winning quartet are Mrs Wood, Miss Neat, Miss Buckingham and Mrs Buckingham.

Special guests at the club's centenary banquet in November 1990 were the Marquess and Marchioness of Tavistock. Also seated are Mr B. White, the town mayor, and Mr C.A. Mitchelmore, the club captain. Standing: Messrs P.J. Parker, D.J. Anthony, R. Bailey, A.C. Rowse, J.R. Wild and B.G. Steer. Basil Speer, the club's long-serving secretary, later became president of the English Golf Union.

The original golf house was built in 1891, and its replacement in 1894. In 1905 it was decided to build new premises and the resultant wood and iron structure is shown here. It was to survive for ten years, before being superseded by a stone building erected a few yards to the north and on the opposite side of Down Road. The latter building formed the basis of the modern clubhouse.

Tavistock's first cinema, in the old cornmarket, opened its doors in 1912. The proprietor, when this picture was taken in 1920, was Clarence Walford. The 'special attraction' in that particular week was a Cecil B. De Mille film. Between 1924 and its closure in 1957 the cinema was operated by Charles Burow.

The Revd Brian Pratt, curate of Tavistock, who married the vicar's sister and became rector of Peter Tavy. In 1927 he was the first man to captain a Tavistock Rugby Club Fifteen. The club played briefly at Abbotsfield and then at Crowndale, but it folded in 1930, not to be revived until 1969.

When the Rugby Club was re-established in 1969 it had no ground. A long period of wandering ended in 1990, when a permanent home was acquired at Sandy Park. Since then there has been a rapid development of activities on and off the field. Here is the team that won the Floodlit Cup in 1991. Back row, left to right: Richard Staniland, Gary Newson, Jim Jefferies, Bayard Peake, Dean Shipton, Aidan Murphy, Toby Neale, Mark Jefferies, Chris Greatrix. Front row: Neil Anderson, Paul Allen, John Wakem, Nick Wakem, Martin Credicott, Barry Hughes, Rob Broome.

Four
Worshipping

The choir of the parish church in 1914. There had been a great deal of controversy in the 1880s, when the vicar of the day, the Revd Walter Tait, had introduced the novelty of the surpliced choir. The acceptance of the innovation seemed to be complete when, in 1906, a new choir vestry was built. On the eve of the First World War the choir gathers round the vicar, the Revd Henry le Neveu. Immediately behind him stands one of his curates, the Revd John Pim. To the left is the Revd Hugh Bickersteth, the other curate, who was to succeed as vicar after the death of Mr le Neveu in 1917.

Constance Bickersteth's pony, 1920. Hugh Bickersteth was vicar from 1918 until his death in 1946. A humble, saintly, otherworldly man, he remained unmarried, but the vicarage was dominated by women. One sister, Constance, was a semi-invalid. The vicar bought her a pony, seen here on the vicarage lawn, but often also to be seen exercising on Whitchurch Down.

Mr and Mrs Clotworthy, c. 1921. The couple were pillars of the church in the early part of the century. William was organist and choirmaster and was a well-known music teacher in the town. He also appears between the two curates on page 53.

The Parish Church from the east, 1914. The church of St Eustachius was dedicated in 1318, and commemorates a second-century Roman martyr. It replaced a small chapel, dedicated to St Matthew, which was the first place of worship in the history of the town.

The Parish Church from the south-east, 1920. Extensive re-building in the fifteenth century, including the addition of the clothworkers' aisle, shown here, reflected the prosperity of the woollen industry in late medieval Tavistock.

Inside St Eustachius, 1903. A major overhaul, conducted in 1844-45, had removed the eighteenth century galleries and pews. Further work, at the end of the century, concentrated on the roof and the floor. An addition in 1903 was the new system of gas lighting, in which floor-based standards were replaced by brass pendants hung from the roof.

The church hall. These premises were acquired by the church in 1911 and substantially rebuilt in 1933. The site, near the top of West Street, had been occupied successively by a Wesleyan meeting house, an elementary school and a school of art. Pictured here in its final decade, the hall was vacated when the new parish centre was opened. It was demolished in 1989.

The cast of a passion play performed in the parish church in the mid 1950s.

A regular event in the Tavistock calendar in the 1950s was youth week. One activity, an inter-club competition, has been won here by the Parish Church Youth Club, whose members display the winning shield. In the centre is the club leader, Thelma Wood.

The Abbey Chapel, *c.* 1905. A survival from the Benedictine Abbey, this building became, in the late-seventeenth century, the first nonconformist meeting house in the town. A Unitarian chapel throughout the nineteenth century, it became, in 1959, a home for the Christian Brethren. A small burial ground is attached.

Congregational Chapel, *c.* 1870. A split between Congregationalists and Unitarians led to the former leaving the abbey chapel and establishing a place of worship on the south side of Brook Street. It was built in 1833. Its first pastor was William Rooker. His congregation was described as 'a little knot of quiet, devout nonconformists'.

Congregational Church, *c.* 1900. Congregationalism grew in Victorian Tavistock. In 1873 a new church was opened on the opposite side of Brook Street to its predecessor. The redundant chapel was pulled down, to provide more space for the market. The new church was to be, for almost a century, an imposing feature of the town landscape. In 1960, the congregation having removed to Russell Street, the building was demolished, and replaced by the Pearl Assurance Company office block.

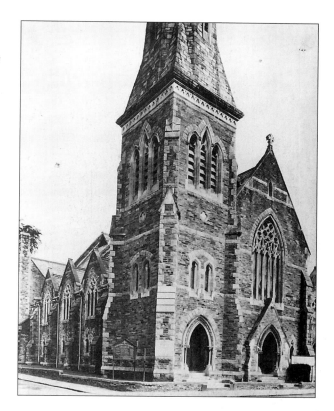

The Brook Street Choir, 1921. Largely through the inspiration of its organist, J. De Blois Rowe, the Congregational church in the early years of the twentieth century established a formidable musical tradition. The church's male voice choir is shown here, possibly on its way to give one of its concerts in Dartmoor Prison. The minister is the Revd W.J. Zeal.

The Russell Street Chapel, 1907. Built in 1838, this chapel accommodated members of the United Methodist Free church, who had broken with mainstream Wesleyanism. In 1960, the two Methodist wings having come together to share the Chapel Street home, the Russell Street chapel offered refuge to the Congregationalists, becoming eventually a United Reformed church.

Members of the Russell Street Chapel, 1906. The setting is a Band of Hope demonstration. In the cause of temperance, 2,000 people from 24 church-based societies marched through the town. A shield, presented to the society that showed 'the greatest originality and taste' in the decoration of a float, was won by the Russell Street Band of Hope. The horse-drawn angel is Miss Muzzlewhite. In the foreground, marshalling the procession, is W.H. Higman, well-known local builder.

The Salvation Army Band in 1925. The most sturdy upholders of the temperance cause have been the soldiers of the Salvation Army. Officers and members of the army band, are shown here. Back row, left to right: Fred Tucker, Len Tucker, Fred Gregory. Middle Row: Sid Dolbear, Fred Crocker, Harry Tucker, William 'Brigham' Young, Bill Tucker, Tom Craze. Seated: Bill Stephens, Joe Gale, Adjutant Devitt, Harry Hoar (bandleader), Captain Mortimore, Howard Hoar, Billy Friend.

A Salvation Army Family, 1940. The army has occupied its citadel on Kilworthy Hill since 1882. For much of its time it has received the support of the Tucker family, six of whom are shown here. Standing: Harry (drums), Len (cornet), Bill (euphonium) and Fred (cornet). Sitting: Nellie and Florrie (songsters).

A Wesleyan Church Bazaar, 1905. The Town Hall had been the venue for the annual Wesleyan bazaar since 1878. The attractions obviously included refreshments. The bearded pastor is, presumably, the Revd Benjamin Broadley, the Wesleyan minister.

The Quaker Meeting House, 1860. This Merrifield photograph offers a glimpse, from across the river, of the plain, stone-built meeting house, on the right of the picture. Built in Dolvin Road in 1836, it was closed in 1870 and demolished in 1879, when its burial ground was incorporated into the adjoining cemetery.

Fitzford Church, *c.* 1900. This huge church, built in the Lombard style by the Duke of Bedford, was designed to meet the needs of the growing population in the western part of the parish. It was opened in 1867. This picture shows its physical dominance over the immediate area, at a time when it was not surrounded by other buildings.

Fitzford Church, 1910. The population of the area, and therefore the congregation of the church, never grew to the anticipated size and closure was to come in 1914. A temporary reopening between 1936 and 1947 was not to offer a solution and the life of the building was only to be saved by an agreement in 1952 to hand it over to the Roman Catholic church.

The gate of the Carmelite Monastery, 1995. This retreat was established in a Victorian house in Watts Road in 1922, when seven nuns arrived from London. Between 1937 and 1952 its chapel was used by the Catholic community outside, who had no other place of worship. In 1995 the five surviving nuns left for a Carmel in Lancashire and the house was closed. The picture was taken on the day of their departure.

The re-dedication of the Whitchurch Bells, 1965. St Andrew's, Whitchurch is a fifteenth century church. Its six bells, hung in 1786 and re-hung in 1896, underwent major renovation in 1965, after which they were re-dedicated by the Bishop of Plymouth, the Rt. Revd Guy Sanderson. To his left are the vicar, the Revd A.R. Gerry, and the captain of the ringers, Mr Harry Mudge.

Five

Caring

This scene was captured in front of the Town Hall in 1912 by Samuel Gimblett, one of the generation of professional photographers to go into business in the years before the First World War. The collecting boxes are labelled 'Cornish Miners' Relief Fund' and the collecting party has arrived complete with barrel organ. There might well have been a sympathetic response to such an appeal in a town that understood at first hand the devastating social effects of a mining depression.

The Union Workhouse at the top of Bannawell Street was opened in 1838. It catered for both a resident body of paupers from the immediate area and a transient population of tramps. Run by a locally elected board of guardians until 1930, it was then taken over by the county council.

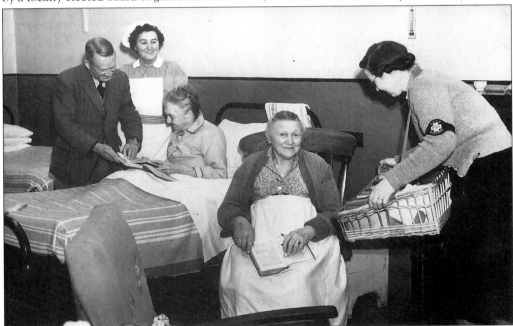

The Workhouse was closed in 1961. For the last few years of its life as a public institution it was known as Gwyntor Hospital. Under the auspices of the local Red Cross, Mr and Mrs Dobbs operated a library there. Here they are, in the 1950s, with two elderly patients. After its closure, the premises were redeveloped and became Russell Court.

The Cottage Hospital is pictured here in 1900, four years after its opening. This was the building in its original form, before the addition, in 1903, of the substantial new wing commemorating John Hornbrook Gill. The hospital replaced an earlier institution which had operated at the foot of Spring Hill since 1887.

In 1890 a London publisher called John Marshall made a gift of property in memory of his wife Ann, who was a native of Tavistock. The result was the appearance, on the Whitchurch Road, of a range of six cottages, to be occupied by local residents who 'from age, ill-health, accident, or infirmity, are unable to maintain themselves by their own exertions'.

The origins of the Tavistock Division of the Red Cross Society lay in a meeting convened in 1910 by the Hon. Mrs Tremayne. The Tremayne family's involvement in the service was commemorated in a cup which bore their name and which was competed for by divisions in the area. Tavistock were the winners in 1931. Their team was, standing: Miss Cranch, Miss Abel, Miss Williams. Sitting: Miss Bellamy, Miss Essery, Miss Elliott, Miss Spurrell.

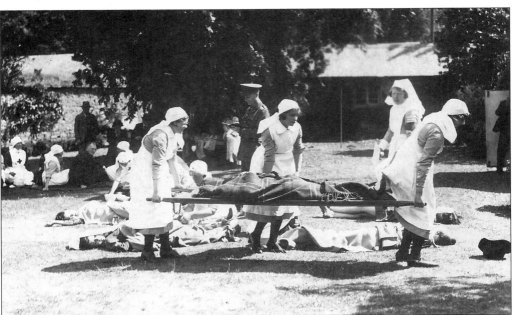

By invitation of its owner, Miss Tremayne, Sydenham House was, in the 1930s, put at the disposal of members of the Red Cross in Tavistock for exercises. Here, in 1934, an emergency arising from an air disaster is simulated.

The Red Cross volunteers providing for older residents in the middle of the Second World War. Smiles, as well as cups of tea, are the order of the day.

The town's permanent memorial of the coronation of Queen Elizabeth II was the Old Folk's Rest Room in Brook Street, formally opened in October 1954. Here, in 1958, surrounded by members and holding on to her dog, is Mrs Dorothea Pinder, the leading figure in this enterprise, as in many other civic activities. She was one of the select band of Honoured Burgesses of Tavistock.

The Tavistock group of the St John's Ambulance Society was inaugurated in 1880. At the end of that year it gave a public display in the Town Hall. Half a century on, the group is celebrating the arrival of a new ambulance, parked here, in 1931, outside its new home in Market Road.

A sizeable turnout of St John's Ambulance personnel to greet a new ambulance in 1948. Standing centre rear, with his head masking the insignia on the side of the vehicle, is Cyril Prance, the county commissioner, a surgeon who was active also in local government. On the far right is Dr Thomas Gillies, for thirty-four years a popular GP in the town until his death in 1968.

Tavistock Fire Brigade outside the fire station in Guildhall Square in 1928. Thomas Brown, superintendent since the beginning of the century, stands fifth from the right on the front row. He also superintended both the waterworks and the markets. The two policemen are PCs Harris and Phare.

Tavistock Fire Brigade outside the fire station in Market Road in 1948. The occasion is the changeover of responsibility from the National Fire Service, operated during the war, to local authority control. Standing sixth from the left is John Philpott, who became station officer four years later and remained so until his retirement in 1974. In recognition of this and other services to the town, he was made an Honoured Burgess of Tavistock in 1996.

Carnival Procession, 1926. Two delivery vans from the laundry at Parkwood take their places among the 137 entries. All the proceeds went to the hospital, as was the case with other carnivals of that period. In spite of the popularity of this particular event it was not repeated until 1932.

Carnival Procession, 1932. The cottage hospital was again the beneficiary. The local Red Cross borrowed a lorry from Perry and Spear, along with a driver, Mr Westcott, and decorated it suitably. The nurses were Miss Toye (standing), Miss Williams, Miss Wargent, Miss Elliott and Miss Cranch (atop). The 'patients' were Girl Guides.

Six

Sharing

The Tavistock Rotary Club was founded in 1925, holding its first lunch on 25 May of that year in the Queen's Head Hotel. Twenty-five years on and a second generation of rotarians, along with a few surviving pioneers, form a group on 8 March 1950. The occasion is a visit by club members to the Westbridge Gasworks. Standing, left to right: Messrs Coulston, Cook, Symons, -?-, Rossington, Jenkins, Martyn, Willis, Quick, Perry, B. Guy, Robbins, Wandless, H. Guy, Middleton, Newnam. Seated: Messrs Doidge, Parriss, Goss, Reeve, Sherman, Swain. Albert Goss, who owned a sweet factory, was chairman of the club. Robert Parriss was manager of the works and host for the day. The Revd Basil Guy was the vicar of Tavistock and was later to become Bishop of Gloucester. Captain Norman Quick was a writer on local subjects. Stanley Jenkins was clerk to the Urban District Council. Others included distinguished representatives of the business and professional life of the town.

For schools and youth groups in the area, the annual Ten Tors competition presents a unique challenge. Here is a 1992 team, representing Tavistock College. Back row, left to right: Tom Balment, Bobby Ancil, Sam Jones, Helen Sloley, Helen Blackburn. Front Row: Heidi Pullybank, Margaret Jennings. Tom was to die tragically in a surfing accident in September 1996.

Scouting came to Tavistock in 1909, a year after the movement had been launched nationally. Here is the local troop in the first year or two of its existence. In the early years Scoutmasters tended to be schoolmasters or curates. The first headquarters were in Old Exeter Road.

A group of Scouts line up at Blanchdown during their Whitsun weekend camp. The year is 1940 and the boys are Fred Brooks, Dennis Crocker, Tony Morcombe, Bert Brooks, Leslie Cornish, Joe Tincombe, Ronald Crocker, Dennis Bishop, Laurence Long and John Sargent.

From the 1950s onwards a major role in the activities of the 1st Tavistock Scout Group has been played by members of the Wassell family. Here, in 1972, Elizabeth and Christopher are flanked by their parents, Harry and Phyllis. They have all held high office in the group and have received national honours in recognition of their work for the movement. Among the changes of the 'Wassell era' was the move, in 1978, into a permanent new headquarters in Pixon Lane.

The Boys' Brigade, founded in 1883, was the pioneer of the uniformed church-affiliated youth organisations. A Tavistock branch had been formed by 1905, in which year it organised this camp, probably on Whitchurch Down.

ALL RANK ABANDON. TOC H YE WHO ENTER HERE.

The lamp of the Tavistock Branch of Toc H was lit by the Prince of Wales in the Albert Hall on 7 December 1927. In the early, pre-war days the branch was strong, as this 1938 picture indicates. Temporary closure during the war was to be followed by re-opening in 1946 and by a visit, in 1951, from the Revd Tubby Clayton, the founder of the movement.

The Womens' Institute has proved to be, in changing times, an enduring feature of the life of small communities. Here, in 1965, the Whitchurch W.I. holds its annual Produce and Handicrafts Show in the village hall. Special guests on this occasion were a number of German visitors from Celle, busily twinning with members of the Tavistock Art Group.

Sharing a harvest festival celebration with members of the Old Folk's Rest Room in October 1981 are the Revd Thomas Smith (Methodist minister), Dee Boyce (secretary), Bill Martin (town clerk), Dorothea Pinder (chairman) and Norma Woodcock (town mayor).

A strong choral tradition existed in the town's schools between the wars. In the 1930s the scholars of Dolvin Road, seen here with A.B. Treloar, their headmaster and choirmaster, regularly won county-wide music competitions.

The scene is the Town Hall in February 1939. The Tavistock Choral Society, founded sixty-one years earlier, is giving a performance of Elgar's *King Olaf*. Standing centre stage, bespectacled, between rostrum and piano, is the conductor, Mr E. Nodder, the long-serving headmaster of the Plymouth Road School. The soloists are Ernest Hargreaves, Mary Bartlett and Watcyn Watcyns and the accompanist is Douglas Durston.

Members of the Townswomen's Guild, in the finery of their Elizabethan costumes, act out their pageant to mark the coronation in 1953. The Tavistock Guild was founded in 1934.

Youth theatre hits Tavistock. The occasion is the first production by The Personalities, a group of entertainers of school age. The group has often performed its own material. The pioneer production, in 1976, was called *Downtown*.

In its first life, from 1922 to 1932, the Operatic Society had concentrated mainly on Gilbert and Sullivan. After its revival, in 1954, its programme became more varied. A lavish production of *The Geisha* in 1962, in the Town Hall, gave full rein to the talents of principals Alfred Brown, Walter Martin, Geoff Richards, Reginald Bawden, Jean Kenzie and Pat Mildren.

In 1981 the Operatic Society again showed its versatility, with *Fiddler on the Roof*. The three sisters featured here are Marilyn Hamshere, Valerie Ling and Alison Mildren.

A production of *The Devil to Pay* by Dorothy L. Sayers in the Barn Theatre at Kelly College in 1952 brought together a number of Tavistock thespians. Back Row: Bernard Reardon, Roy Johns, Olive Johns, Edith Frise, Leonard Stanbury, Joan Gliddon, Lilian Crout, Fred Horrell, George Neale, George Fitze, Michael Kelly. Front Row (from centre): Pat Hillson, Norman Condy, Ethel Rundle-Wood, Edith Down, Elsie Horrell, Pretoria Walters, Fernley Frise, Philip Perry. Kneeling, John Spear, Arthur Vigers. The producer was Eric Kingdon.

The Tavonians were launched in 1935. No one has appeared in more of its productions than Philip Perry, who joined the society in 1948. He is shown here as Canon Chasuble, alongside Jean Lopez's Miss Prism, in the 1986 production of *The Importance of Being Earnest*.

On 30 June 1923, Mrs Gallie opened the grounds of her home, Littlecourt, for a folk dance festival. The house, designed by Sir Edwin Lutyens, was the first to be built in Down Road. It was badly damaged by fire in 1947. The energetic and enterprising Mrs Gallie was also the secretary of the Tavistock Badminton Club.

Members of the Tavistock Folk Dance Club became established ambassadors for the town in the 1980s, with their twinning visits. Here they dance down the main shopping street in Pontivy, on the occasion of its biennial fair. The club has also organised a popular series of Folk Dance Festivals for young children, held annually in the Pannier Market, which have involved a large number of schoolchildren from Tavistock and the surrounding area.

Seven

Learning

The Grammar School in Russell Street was opened in 1837, the year of Queen Victoria's accession. Its longest-serving headmaster, for a record thirty-five years, was the Revd Edward Spencer. Spencer retired in 1888, in his seventieth year. The occasion was marked by a gathering of pupils and ex-pupils and by the presentation of 'a silver tea and coffee set, a richly chased and engraved silver salver, and a handsome timepiece under a glass shade'. The young men around him include Edward Chilcott, seated third from the left, who partnered his father in the local law firm, captained the Tavistock cricket team and was later to be councillor and magistrate. Only one old boy has forgotten to remove his hat. Behind him the wire-netting covering the window is a reminder of the necessity at that time to protect windows against the late-Victorian mania among the young for stone-throwing.

After the Revd Spencer's retirement the Russell Street School was closed and the Grammar School was re-opened in new buildings on Plymouth Road. Here, the school is recorded in 1921. The staff are Miss M. Balkwill, Messrs E.W. Wallis, J.J. Alexander (headmaster), R.C. Sleep and C. Hartley. The masters were nicknamed 'Joey', 'Junket', 'Sleepy', and 'Froggy'.

The Grammar School First Eleven in 1930. Back Row, left to right: Mr L.H. Woollett, W.C. Philp, L.H. Lee, P. Holmes, L.G. Welsford, H. Symons, H.T. Treloar, Mr H.B. Smith. Middle Row: M.J. Coleman, L.W. Workman, A.B. Treloar (captain), P.J. Coleman, F.W. Steed. Front Row: S.W. Colling, G.G. Hill. The record in that season was playing ten games and winning ten.

Alexander's School in Plymouth Road had, by 1932, outgrown its premises and in that year it moved to new accommodation at Crowndale. The building is shown here in 1950, with its wartime additions of temporary classrooms and its well-remembered sports pavilion.

Grammar School Corps Band, *c.* 1935. Centrally seated is the headmaster, G. Irving Gass. To his left sits Sergeant Dingley, one half of the husband and wife team that provided caretaking, cooking and other services to the school.

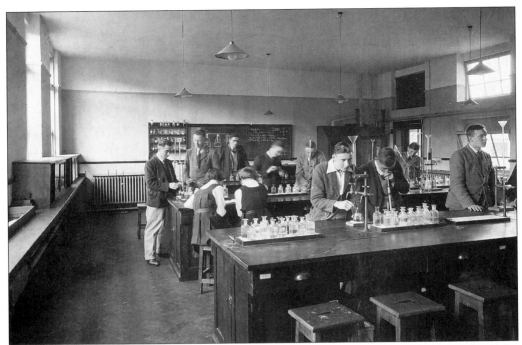

This photograph was taken in the late 1940s, as one of a series of publicity photographs of the school and shows the chemistry laboratory and a group of senior pupils, including two girls. Girls had first been admitted in 1932, when the new building was opened.

The Headmaster K.D. Anderson outside the front door of the school in 1949 with his prefects. They are, standing: Gerald Olver, Margaret Dawe, Fred Sherrell, Ann Myers and Richard Wheatley. Sitting: John Puddifoot, Dennis Penny, Brenda Collins and Celia Moore.

The school choir in 1949. Mrs Verrall's impressively large group includes, second from the left on the back row, James Metcalf, headmaster of the school thirty years later.

School sports day in 1952. Amid scenes of unrestrained enthusiasm, Mr Hartley prepares to fire.

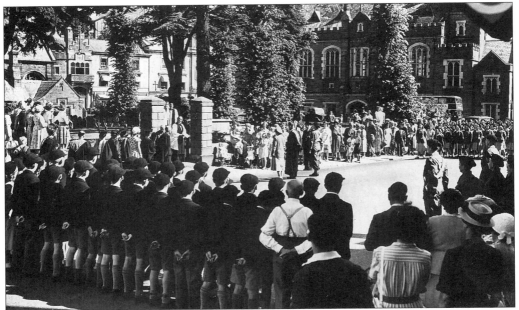

On 25 July 1952 the school celebrated the 400th anniversary of its re-constitution following the closure of the abbey and the monastic school. A service was held in the parish church at which the Bishop of Exeter gave an address. The scene outside St Eustachius is here observed from the steps of the Bedford Hotel.

Whitchurch Primary School, ninety years after its foundation, shows off its class of 1965. Back row, left to right: Sally Jackman, Ian Chappell, Linda Cox, William Seager, Judith Hitchen, Ronald Whatton, Andrew Seager, Veronica Larson, Paul Williams, Susan Toye, Paul Perkin, Teresa Mudge. Third Row: John Rowe, Valerie Toye, Jeremy Bartlett, Mervyn Burridge, Shirley Jackman, Roger Densham, Wendy Toye, Derek Cruze, Ann Seager, John Haytor, Wendy C. Toye, Mark Williams, Martin Roberts, Peter Heath. Second Row: Michael Burridge, John King, Clare Haytor, Andrew Watkins, Sandra Bray, Philip Maker, Wendy King, Stephen Seager, Shirley Toye, Graham Burridge, Linda Toye, Tim Larsen, Angela Larsen, Scott Eslick, Geraldine Perkin, Ian Doidge. Front Row: Frances Brewer, David Rowe, Christine Cox, Sandra Burridge, Kevin Bartlett, Janet Watkins, Ian Densham, Shirley Burridge. Miss Alford on the left and Mrs West on the right are the teachers.

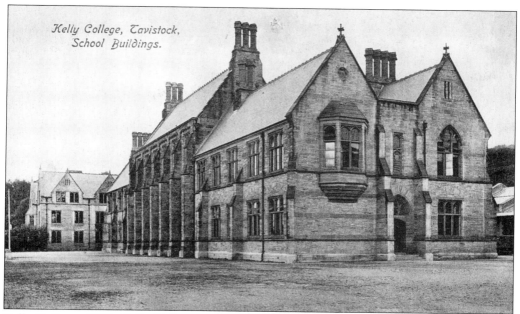

Kelly College, 1917. Kelly College was founded in 1877, as a result of a bequest of Admiral Benedictus Marwood Kelly. The admiral's first considerations were to provide boarding education for his own descendants and for the orphan sons of naval officers, but it developed the wider features of a Victorian public school.

Kelly College Library, 1917. Although the school had retained its boarding provision as a fundamental characteristic, it had already by that date reached out to the local community by taking day boys. Girls were not accepted until 1972.

The Dolvin Road School was built in 1847. This picture, taken in front of the infants' classroom, dates from 1918. The pupils are, back row, left to right: Emily Harry, Cissy Golding, -?-, Sybil Morris, Dorothy Vincent, Muriel Cornish. Middle Row: Gladys Tucker, -?-, Barbara Arthurs, Motee Hoar, Violet McCabe, -?-, Judy Babbidge. Front Row: Mary Wiggins, Edith Pooley, -?-, Barbara Hutchins, Cissy Hutchins, Gladys Balsdon, -?-, Nora Gale.

The headmaster of Dolvin Road between 1920 and 1946 was A.B. Treloar. He had many talents and interests and appeared to bequeath them equally among his six children. They surround him in this 1930 picture. Standing are sons Harry, Bray and Hugh. Sitting to the side of Mrs Treloar is Douglas and in front of her is Charles. Joyce sits by her father.

May Revels, 1926. This annual ceremony, associated with the Dolvin Road school, dates back to 1921. In the early years only the girls participated, the boys being spectators. A procession, with a series of floral dances, accompanied the May Queen to the vicarage garden, where the coronation took place. Dancing and displays followed.

May Revels, 1947. To the admiring looks of boys behind the garden bushes, Audrey Weeks, the May Queen and to her right Peggy Bowhay, her successor, take the centre-stage at the ceremony in the vicarage garden, after being carried from the school on a flower-decked lorry.

The staff of Dolvin Road, 1956. After the Second World War, Dolvin Road became a secondary school. Here the headmaster, Edward Richardson, sits alongside the bespectacled exchange teacher from America, Forrest Askey. Flanking the pair are, on the left: Mrs E. Brennan, Miss I. Martin and Miss E. Workman and, on the right: Mrs E. Brown, Miss H. White and Mrs S. Parsons. Standing: Messrs L. Quirk, A. Brown, R. Maddison, E. Hopkins, R. Stock, T. Brown, A. Helm and A. Cook.

The County Primary School, long housed on Plymouth Road, moved into a new Crowndale home in 1991. In November of that year the school added a novel feature to its surroundings in the form of a time-line depicting a series of events over a long time span. On the right is one of the period-costumed pupils, Jennifer Lea. On the left is County History Adviser Chris Taylor. In the centre is Roz Wates, designer of the pavement.

Eight
Governing

The first Tavistock Urban District Council was elected in 1898. In April 1948, to mark its golden jubilee, members and officials gathered for the camera. Back row, left to right: A. Pethick, S.C. Willis, H. Moore, W.E. Colson (surveyor), W.T. Reeve, A.D. Lowe, L.C. Tovey, E.D. Allen-Price (medical officer of health), C.B. Lacey (treasurer), S.R. Goode, W.C. Rawling, F.G. Quant. Front Row: E.E. Kerswill, O.S. Johnstone, S.G. Jenkins (clerk), J. Heyden, G.G. Pearce, M.E. Bazley, G.A. Knott. The civic maces were a gift made in 1761 to the town by the Duke of Bedford.

The most powerful agency of local government before the establishment of the Urban District Council was the Bedford Estate Office. The family itself lived at faraway Woburn, but in 1810 they had built, a few miles out of the town, a Tamarside 'cottage' which was called Endsleigh and which is pictured here a century on. Essentially a holiday home, it proved to be a useful base from which a duke could make an occasional inspection of his local estates.

William Winney was the first chairman of the Urban District Council and was photographed at the time of his appointment in 1898. A Wesleyan preacher and a radical, he was master of a small school on Spring Hill that later became an annexe to the hospital. He was one of the first of the 129 people who were to sit on the council during the 68 years of its life.

Joseph Heyden, chairman of the UDC, aboard a 'Westcountry' class locomotive of the Southern Railway, which he has just named after the town, June 1947. This is an example of the ceremonial duties expected of a chairman. Joseph Heyden was a retired schoolmaster who was much involved in the public life of the town during and after the Second World War.

Archie Mill, the UDC chairman, on the right, and his Pontivy counterpart Marcel Lambert, conduct the formalities that established the twinning, October 1958. Mr Mill was a watchmaker. For thirty years the town depended on him to wind and maintain the town clock.

The Civic Ball tradition began in 1953 and soon became established as a high point in a chairman's term of office. George Gerald Pearce, surrounded here by other notables at the 1963 ball, was a founding partner of a well-known firm of solicitors. The council clerk, Stanley Jenkins, is, as usual, at his shoulder, while fellow councillors Wilf Rawling and Tom Brown also appear in the group.

Local government re-organisation that brought an end to the UDC led to a division of local responsibilities between a town and a district council. Seen here on a cold December evening in 1991 are the two civic heads, Mike Warren, the town mayor, on the left and Roy Cook, the borough mayor, on the right. In the middle is the local MP, Emma Nicholson. The occasion is the Dickensian evening, an event held annually from 1984.

Among those to have represented Tavistock in parliament was John Pym, who led the parliamentary campaign against Charles I. On 6 December 1943, the tercentenary of his death, Isaac Foot delivered an address at the foot of the Duke's statue, paying tribute also to the Bedfords, who, he said, had shared Pym's political views. Standing at the back, wearing the trilby, is Isaac's son Michael, later to be a cabinet minister and leader of the Labour Party.

Electioneering in the 1960s. Grenville Jones, the Liberal candidate in the 1964 General Election, canvasses support. He failed to dislodge the sitting Conservative member, Sir Henry Studholme. Two years later Sir Henry retired and Michael Heseltine became MP for the constituency.

John Spear, a yeoman farmer with Milton Abbot roots, won the Tavistock seat in the General Election of 1900. He had this picture taken of himself in front of his home, 'Venn' in the parish of Lamerton, just before the 1906 election, when he sought re-election and lost. He was to lose again in January 1910.

When John Spear re-gained the seat in December 1910, his Conservative supporters organised a notable victory demonstration. A total of 390 people, representing the size of his majority, armed themselves with miniature spears, greeted the new member at the top of Launceston Road, and formed a procession which included the Brentor Brass Band. A landau drawn by six greys, with postillions and outriders, bore the victor into town. The cavalcade made its way to Bedford Square via Plymouth Road and the band played *See the Conquering Hero Come*.

Nine

Trading

The northern side of Bedford Square in 1858. The scene captured here disappeared within months, to be replaced by the new Duke Street and Bedford Square. The drapery business of Charles Bawden was taken over by James Mayston and later by Edward Yelland. The premises of the other two businesses featured here were demolished as part of the re-development. John Tanton's drapery store disappeared, as did the Railway Inn, whose proprietor, Mrs Caroline Luke, moved across the river to take over the new Cattle Market Inn on Whitchurch Road. The Railway Inn had, in 1858, only recently changed its name from the Plymouth Inn, in preparation for the imminent arrival of the Great Western Railway.

John Carter was born in 1848. His mother brought up her family of five on her own after her husband had, like many others, gone to America and forgotten to come back. In 1881 John went into the grocery business and ran a store which in 1913 he passed on to his daughter Winifred and her new husband Henry Creber. In April 1928, following a fire, John, on his eighty-first birthday, laid the foundation stone of the newly extended premises. He died two months later. The store formally remained Carter's for some time, but its future was to lie under another name. For generations of shoppers, Creber's Corner was to be one of the most familiar spots in town.

Herbert Brown established his business in Brook Street in 1915 and traded there until the late 1920s. The size of the staff, seen here towards the end of the period, is an indication of how labour-intensive such trades were in those days.

A part of Brown's business, which he bought from John Barkell, was a milk delivery service. This operated twice daily. Other dairy items were sold, delivered or despatched by post. Deliveries in 1915 depended on the horse.

By the mid-1920s the Brown business boasted a smart delivery van. It also extended its accommodation and began to offer refreshment facilities. It had, nevertheless, ceased to trade by 1930 and the premises had become a barber's shop.

H.W Skinner, *c.* 1908. Up to the eve of the First World War, Hugh William Skinner ran a family business at 25 West Street, which had been operating since before the 1840s. It was, in 1908, one of eight butchers' shops in the town.

Lennards, 1923. This shoe shop was established near the bottom of West Street just before the First World War. It is hoped that the person who adjusted the sign to the swimming baths so that it pointed up West Street rather than King Street will now, at last, own up.

Williams and Son, 1915. Established in the 1870s, this firm of painters and decorators, at 24 Market Street, was still there in 1939.

J.E. Symons, *c.* 1904. John England Symons stands rather stiffly on the step of his shop in Duke Street, which he has occupied since the 1880s. He has just acquired a second shop in West Street, in which, from 1912, he was to concentrate his business.

Richard Northcott Stranger came from Holsworthy to Tavistock, where, in 1898, he took over a draper's shop in Market Street on the death of its owner William Winter. In 1912 he moved into these premises in Pym Street, previously occupied by Charles Harris. This picture and the one below, show the Stranger emporium in about 1930.

Manchester House, between the wars, housed the most substantial drapery business in the town. It did not, however, survive Mr Stranger's death in 1937.

John German founded, in the 1870s, a family business that traded on until the eve of the Second World War. Its premises, on the corner of Market Street, are shown here in about 1930. Boot and shoe makers, the firm was particularly proud of the 'Dartmoor', which it advertised as 'the strongest boot in the world'.

The interior of the only chemist's shop in Tavistock in 1930. This was the business of Doble and Son at 5 Duke Street, then being run by William Burnage. It was soon to be sold to Boots. The chair, for waiting customers, remained a welcome facility in many shops until recent times.

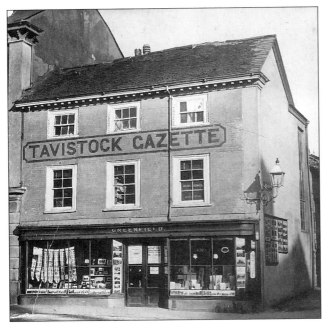

George Spencer, bookseller and stationer, launched the *Tavistock Gazette* in 1857 and for nine years published it from his small shop in Market Street. Then he moved into larger premises on the north side of Bedford Square. Thomas Greenfield took over the business and the editorship of the paper, from him in 1874. Part of the original Bedford Square building was sliced off to accommodate the new Drake Road. What remained is shown here, as it appeared in 1905. Two years later, towards the end of Greenfield's term as editor, new premises, comprising editorial offices and printing works, were built in Pym Street.

In 1974 the *Tavistock Gazette* was closed and the Pym Street property was vacated. This is the composing room shortly before closure. The building was subsequently overhauled and given a new function as a community centre. Its new name, Kingdon House, commemorated the last of the six editors of the old broadsheet. Eric Kingdon was one year older than the building. He edited the paper from 1954 to 1974. The old paper's title was later resurrected and added to that of its erstwhile competitor, to produce the masthead *Tavistock Times Gazette*.

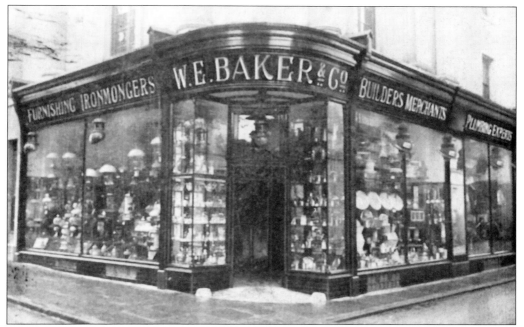

W.E. Baker launched his business in the 1860s. It survived for more than a century. This is what the premises, on a prime town-centre site, on the corner of North Street, looked like in about 1920.

The lower part of West Street as it appeared in about 1950. On the right is the business established just before the war by William Fellowes, the former professional footballer. On the left is the butcher's shop that was run, successively, by four generations of the Willis family, who coined the advertising slogan, 'Meat makes mites mighty'. On the same side of the road is London House, a tailoring establishment, previously run by Williams and Snell and then by Frank Naish. Here, in 1950, it forms an addition to the premises of Sweet and Son across the road.

In 1822 the building then known as Abbey House was converted to become the Bedford Hotel. It has since maintained its position as the town's principal hotel. In 1895, when this picture was taken, it not only offered the range of services associated with a hostelry, but also provided facilities for receptions, balls and public meetings. It remained part of the property of the Bedford estate until 1955.

The Kerswill family ran a building business from Taylor Square and were responsible for a large number of the public and private buildings erected in the first half of the twentieth century. Four generations of the family face the camera in 1900. On the right is George, aged seventy-two. On the left is his son James, the founder of the firm. James is the father of William, who holds his first-born, Tom. Baby Tom did not join the firm, but opted for a naval career followed by some years as a postman in Tavistock.

Ten
Travelling

Ford Street, *c.* 1870. The street was so named because it gave access to the ford at the point where West Bridge was later built. By the middle of the nineteenth century this road had replaced Whitchurch Road as the main route out to Plymouth. Like all the other main roads out of the town, it was taken over by a turnpike trust, which maintained it and charged tolls for its use. A number of tollhouses on the edge of the town have survived. This one hasn't. Its function ended in 1867 after the demise of the trust that operated it. It was demolished towards the end of the century to improve access to West Bridge.

West Bridge was built in the middle of the sixteenth century. Originally ten feet wide, it was widened by a further twelve feet a century later. It was demolished in 1940 and replaced by the single-span bridge that now carries the main Plymouth Road.

A public road transport system to serve the area was developed between the wars. As this mid-twenties glimpse through Court Gate shows, the buses used Bedford Square as terminus and staging-point.

The pupils of the Tavistock High School for Girls, an academy for young ladies operated in Glanville Road by Mr and Mrs A.J. Huckle, climb aboard the *Tavy Queen* en route for Bude. The charabanc was operated by Matthews and Company, as here in 1920, from their Drake Road garage. An earlier form of transport has left its mark.

A day out in 1919. The starting point is the Duke of York, which had been converted from a private house to an inn in the 1850s. The date and the faces suggest that this might have been an ex-servicemen's outing, conceivably by members of the local branch of 'The Comrades of the Great War', the forerunner of the British Legion.

The Walkham Viaduct in 1892. One of the masterpieces of the great engineer I.K. Brunel, this viaduct was constructed to carry the Great Western Railway line over the river, between Horrabridge and Tavistock. It was 367 yards long and 132 feet high. A timber superstructure was built on a range of tall stone pillars. The line was opened in 1859.

The G.W.R. station, as it appeared soon after its opening in 1859. Looking from the Whitchurch end, the goods yard is on the left. The original wooden station was burned down in 1887 and replaced in stone. In 1889, some 2,000 people gathered here to hear Mr Gladstone make a brief speech from the open window of his carriage as his train paused on its way to Plymouth.

In 1865 the line from Plymouth to Tavistock was extended northwards to Lydford and then to Launceston. It is shown here, in about 1920, as it leaves the town, accompanying both the river and the road along the valley. In the foreground is the Tavy Iron Foundry. Overlooking the houses and small factories of Parkwood is Kelly College.

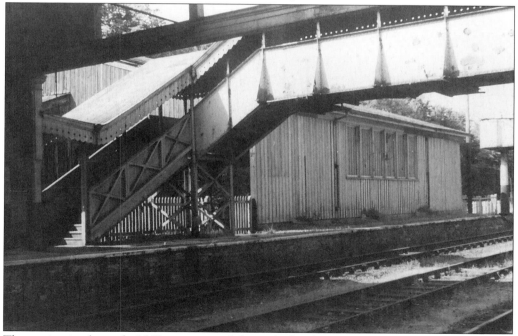

The station in the early 1960s as it neared the end of its life. The line closed on 29 December 1962, an occasion marked by a blizzard that prevented the last two scheduled trains from running.

The G.W.R.'s competitor, the London and South Western Railway, opened its line through Tavistock in 1890. The station site is shown here with construction work still going on. Above and to the left are the cottages of Trelawny Road. Sir John Trelawny had been MP for Tavistock for seventeen years in the middle of the century.

The nature of the local terrain meant that the engineers of the new line were faced with major problems. The challenge of spanning the valley from Kilworthy Hill to Glanville Road was met by the construction of a viaduct, which is seen here in the first year of its life. Twenty years after the closure of the line, the viaduct was reopened as a walkway.

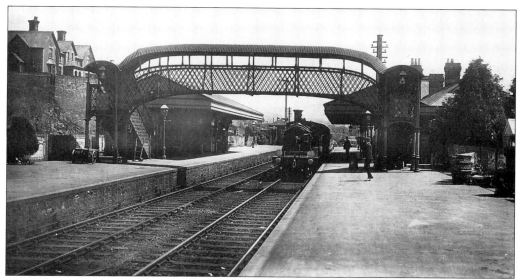

The L.S.W.R. station in 1915. While the G.W.R. route through Tavistock was a branch line, the L.S.W.R. track was the company's main line from Waterloo, through Exeter and Oke-hampton and on to Plymouth.

The view from the L.S.W.R. station in 1924. For many visitors, this must have been the first impression of Tavistock. Many of the features of the centre of town have remained unchanged, although it is noticeable that in the 1920s little development had taken place across the river.

The L.S.W.R. station bedecked for the 1937 coronation. Standing to attention is Frank Quant, a councillor of long standing, who was made an Honoured Burgess in recognition of his public service and whose name was to be given to a small estate built on the site of the redundant station.

In May 1897 a goods train was derailed and wrecked on the L.S.W.R. line between Tavistock and Brentor. There was no loss of life, but the accident was costly. The *Tavistock Gazette* reported that 'The heaped up and broken waggons presented a rather appalling spectacle'. One can imagine the child in the picture dining-out for many years to come on stories of the scene.

Eleven

Confronting

The Territorial Army was established in 1908. In Tavistock, an Infantry Batallion of the Devonshire Regiment was set up, based at the Drill Hall on Rocky Hill. At the same time, the 223rd Battery, 56th (Wessex) Brigade was founded, with its headquarters at Crelake Barracks. The latter was commanded in 1923, when this picture was taken, by Major Kenneth Brown, seated here behind the shield won in a shooting competition. The other officer, on his right, is W.C. Perry, partner in the coal and builder's merchants Perry, Spear and Company.

In 1909 permission was given, rather reluctantly, for a Territorial Army Camp to be held on Whitchurch Down. The powerful Commoners' Association insisted on a set of strict conditions and the army was faced with a bill for £3 for the two-week camp, together with costs of twelve shillings for the supervision of the commoners' cattle and five shillings for tidying up afterwards.

Mounted troops in Duke Street in 1914. It is not clear whether they are regular soldiers or members of the yeomanry. If the latter, they belong to the Tavistock Troop, A-Squadron, of the Royal North Devon Hussars, commanded by Lieut. the Hon H.B. Money-Coutts. This was the cavalry element of the new Territorial Army.

Sergeant Percy Hodge, Number 1112, Third Section, Wessex Divisional Ammunition Column, is here to represent the 751 men from the parishes of Tavistock and Whitchurch who fought in the First World War. On 5 September 1915 he wrote home from Lyndhurst Camp with this picture of himself and the message 'Just a card to let you know that I am still alive and well'.

In 1916 the stately home of Mount Tavy, imposingly situated to the north-east of the town, was converted into a neurological hospital. Here, nearly 1,000 battle-scarred patients were treated for shell-shock and other disorders, the bulk of them by therapy that involved work in agriculture, carpentry and handicraft. The hospital is seen here in 1919, in its final days. The premises have, in recent years, accommodated Mount House school.

Having dressed up in carnival spirit, this group, posing outside the market, prepares to raise money on Comrades' Day. A local branch of the Comrades of the Great War had been formed in 1918 and here, in the following year, it holds its first collection day. As the organisation developed into the British Legion, so the occasion evolved into Poppy Day.

The original plan for a war memorial to occupy a site at the corner of the churchyard was abandoned on grounds of cost and Guildhall Square was finally chosen. The granite monument is seen here at its inauguration on 21 May 1921. A total of 119 names were inscribed. A further 40 were to be added after the Second World War.

During the Second World War, Red Cross volunteers undertook the operation of distributing food parcels. Here, they are on their rounds collectiong items of tinned food.

The spring of 1941 brought the height of the aerial assault on Plymouth. Many refugees from the blitz arrived in Tavistock, having fled the city. Some were accommodated in private homes, although billets were few because of the arrival of evacuees. Public buildings were pressed into service. Many slept either under the skies or in the most temporary of shelters.

Plaisterdown Camp in 1950. Some three miles to the east of Tavistock, between Whitchurch and Sampford Spiney, lies a stretch of open moorland. It once looked like this. The camp was built in 1943 by the American military authorities to house a hospital. In the period following D-Day it operated flat out. After the war the camp was used by the services. Its last duty was as a receiving point for Ugandan Asians thrown out by Idi Amin in 1972.

Members of 2312 Squadron Air Training Corps in 1965. Their home was then Crelake Barracks. They later moved to the Drill Hall and then to Tavistock School. The seated officers include Flt. Lt. Arthur Ball, the founder of the squadron in 1953, who is second from the right, and his successor, Flt. Lt. Roy Skipworth, who sits third from the left. Also featured are Flying Officers Treadgold (second from left) and Gardner (far right).

Twelve

Celebrating

George Henry Anthony was, during the 1930s, the G.W.R. stationmaster at Tavistock. He was also a member of the choral society, of the church choir and, from 1935, of the Urban District Council. When arrangements for King George V's jubilee were being discussed, he, as a former resident of Helston, suggested that a Furry Dance be included in the programme. It proved so popular that two years later, in 1937, it was again incorporated in a town celebration, this time of the coronation of King George VI. This is the coronation day scene on a rather grey May morning in Duke Street.

Edward VIII visited the town three times as Prince of Wales and once as King. In 1918 he called in on the Mount Tavy military hospital. In 1919, as recorded here, he inspected the Kelly College Officers' Training Corps. In 1921 he visited the cottage hospital and the county show at Crowndale. In 1936 he made a brief stop in Bedford Square.

Another part of the programme of events on the occasion of George VI's coronation was the organisation of public tea parties in the Pannier Market.

Princess Elizabeth visited the town on 22 October 1949. She wore a double-breasted, full skirted, cloth coat of royal blue with a slim-fitting waistline, an off-the-face hat trimmed with an osprey feather to tone, and a triple row of pearls. She was welcomed by Council Chairman Mr Stanley Willis and later chatted to some schoolchildren in the crowd.

In 1977 the Prince of Wales paid a visit to Kelly College on the occasion of the school's centenary. Shaking his distinguished guest's hand is Graham Willis, the town mayor. Twenty-eight years earlier his father had greeted the prince's mother. Now, for a second time, a Willis welcomes a Windsor.

Tavistock Goose Fair is one of only two fairs in the country to identify themselves in name with the long-necked honker. The other is at Nottingham. Originally known as the Michaelmas Fair, it became an established feature of the Tavistock calendar in the middle of the sixteenth century. It was then one of five annual fairs. As a major popular event attracting both residents and visitors, it outlived its four contemporaries. Here is a section of the crowd outside the cattle market at the 1905 fair. The Cattle Market Inn, then run by Alice Gidley, is on the left.

Bedford Square on Goose Fair Day, 1920. In its early years, the fair was celebrated on the feast day of St Michael, 29 September. The present practice of holding it on the second Wednesday in October was adopted in 1822. By the end of the nineteenth century it was reckoned that the number of visitors, many arriving by train, exceeded the size of the resident population.

Carnival, 1909. The first Tavistock carnival was held on 5 November 1885. It consisted of a torchlit procession which marked Guy Fawkes night but ranged much more widely in its themes. This was still the pattern in 1909, when this interesting group formed one of the tableaux. Charities benefitted. The Tavistock soup kitchen was the most regular beneficiary.

The carnival was revived after the First World War, without the Guy Fawkes link. The practice then became established of giving all the proceeds to the hospital. During the twenties, as this picture from the beginning of the decade shows, the procession formed up in Market Road. In the foreground is the Salvation Army float with a harvest festival theme. After a gap from 1926 to 1932 the tradition was revived in 1932 with a 190-entry extravaganza.

Whitham Park is a 40-house estate developed by the Urban District Council in the late 1920s. Like many streets of similar age, it had, by the time of the Second World War, a large number of young families. In 1945, again like countless estates, it celebrated the end of the war in Europe with an open-air V.E. street party. Similar parties were to form part of the celebrations for the Queen's coronation eight years later.

Celebrations can be part of national occasions, like coronations. They can equally mark local events, such as town fairs. At a third level they can mark the passage of time in the lives of organisations and societies. Here is a typical example of the latter. Perraton's, the town centre confectioners and caterers, are preparing to serve members of the Bowling Club, gathered for their annual dinner in the Red Barn, off Kilworthy Hill. The year is 1953.